The Art Of War Within

Paul Justin Tiemujin Ramirez

I dedicate this book to my daughter Noelle and my son Ryan.

If you compare yourself with or seek approval from others, you will surely lose your way. May evil, fear, suffering, tragedy, and temptation remain masterless over your lives, and, may you live your lives masterfully.

"If some years were added to my life,
I would dedicate 50 years to study the book of Changes,
And then, I might come to be without great fault."

-Confucius

At Age 70

Author's Note

My work below on "The Book of Changes" prompts me to offer a modest complement to Sun-Tzu's immortal treatise on "The Art of War." Sun-Tzu admonishes us to "know thy enemy, know thyself, and in one hundred battles you will not fail." His admonition implicitly acknowledges that mastery of war requires mastery of oneself. I would only add that mastery of anything in this life, including oneself, is attained only through trial and tribulation. Mastery therefore requires time, repetition, revision, and correction. Most of all, mastery requires embracing failure, whether that failure is of one's own making or is encountered by observing someone else's.

Nothing encountered in life is ultimately singular or simple. All of life's challenges contain multitudes, and therefore the challenges in life offer a myriad of missteps that arise unseen only after the journey has begun. This is the reason why too many of life's journeys end in despair. I offer the following maxim to aid in my own and in my readers' future journeys:

Know yourself, know The Book of Changes, and after one hundred setbacks you will find your Dao.

知己知易經, 百磨你得道

Contents

Acknowledgements

Preface

Introduction

How to Use This Book

The 64 Epigrams

Acknowledgments

I would like to express my deep gratitude to three most important persons; without their support and insight this book would not have been possible. First is my revered high school American History teacher, Mr. Jim Thompson; I would have never developed such a deep interest in learning or searching for knowledge had it not been for you.

Second, my Chinese language teachers, Catherine Li and Katie Roller from Chapman University who started me on this journey. Dr. Youli Sun, Lixin Meng, Lizi Qing, and Joyce Li from Peking University's Classical Studies Department (China Studies Institute) who understood what I was searching for and bombarded me with so much classical Chinese literature that I broke out with dyshidrotic eczema. Dr. Qingyun Wu, former Coordinator of the Chinese Language Program at Cal State University Los Angeles, who guided and guarded me towards the completion of my academic goals.

Last but not least, my family, friends from the US Army, and The Genesis House Rancho Park Recovery Center. I am forever grateful.

Preface

Sometime after the war, after returning from China in 2012, I found myself in rehab heartbroken over a relationship I knew had overrun its course. Months before then something had told me it was time to leave but for some reason I hadn't listened. I had consulted the I-CHING about what I should do and it had told me what I did not want to hear. It gave me hexagram 33 with changing line 4 which reads: "If you recognize the moment for RETREAT, be certain that you do it with the proper attitude-that is, willingly. In this way you will adjust easily and progress in your new environment. Those who are filled with emotional turmoil during withdrawal will suffer greatly." I ended up staying in the relationship and finding out the hard way that I was being cheated on. The I-Ching was right, and my attempt to ignore its teaching only caused more pain. I should have popped smoke when I had the chance.

My experience in rehab taught me that betrayal hurts just as much as a hangover or withdrawal from alcohol. In rehab, I was allowed to take one item with me and that one thing I chose was my I-Ching workbook by R.L. Wing. I had not picked up or opened the I-Ching in four years. I spent the two months looking out the window of my recovery house overlooking Cheviot Hills Recreation Center and reading the I-Ching over and over again. At the same time, I listened to people with behavioral disorders and with severe drug and alcohol addiction problems. To me this place was an abyss, like being trapped in purgatory and the only positive spin I could put on it was remembering what John Milton said, "The mind is its own place and, in itself can make a heaven of hell or a hell of heaven."

Next to my friends in the Army, these people would become some of the best friends I have ever made. They reminded me of Nietzche when he said - "The great epochs of our life are the occasions when we gain the courage to rebaptize our evil qualities as our best qualities." They expressed themselves openly, honestly, and proudly; they were motivating, beyond funny, and borderline insane. These qualities most of all made them realistic about life, money, and relationships. They were interesting because it was like they lived on the border-line between this world and the next. These people had experienced suffering on multiple levels and had successfully recovered from addiction and then relapsed multiple times, only to continue to come back and try again. I admired their resilient and relentless spirits to want to make attempt after attempt to do the right thing, to get their life right, in my opinion to try to find their Dao even if they knew it was going to end in oblivion.

Part of the Art of War Within's inspiration for me came from my experience with my fellow addicts in rehab. I attended certain meetings with them three times a day, meetings that required the participant to stand and recite: "My name is Paul Ramirez, and I am an alcoholic." Although I am not a psychologist, this kind of negative affirmation was very difficult for me to engage in. To me, it constituted an anchor that bound me to a system meant to give me a lifetime label and to keep me down and dependent on endless meetings with stale literature. The other part of the rehabilitation was a requirement to attend an outpatient clinic once a day. Each day offered a different type of counselor with her own style of treatment. The person whose philosophy resonated with me and the I-Ching most was a therapist named Gianina. She was kind, intelligent, on top of that she was beautiful, and she in fact made me forget my ex-girlfriend. Her approach consisted of the mantra "things don't happen to you, they happen through you."

Since I was a child I had been drawn to the Warrior Culture. As a kid during Halloween, I alternated each year between ninja or commando costumes. While most high schoolers were concerned with their SAT scores and which college they were going to attend, I was planning to go to the Army in search of adventure and to create my personal legend. My imagined future mirrored the movie narratives that I grew up watching: the young hero that hears a calling and goes off to become an elite soldier, fights in a war, and somewhere along the line develops deadly supernatural fighting skills that he then takes back home to save his small home town from trouble, only to find out that HE is the source of the trouble. That hero had left war only to re-encounter it at home and within himself.

At age 19 I found myself jumping out of planes and kicking open doors to support America's "war on terror." For me it was the first time I could be me and not get in trouble for it. I didn't have to think, I just did. And where I was was where I wanted to be. I was intoxicated with the combination of excitement and fear of being blown to pieces before a mission, and then filled with testosterone and the adrenaline of success after completing it. For that short time I was within my "Dao" or maybe within just a part of my Dao. Ernest Hemingway once wrote, "There is no hunting like the hunting of man, and those who have hunted armed men long enough and liked it, never care for anything else thereafter." I can say that for a short time in my life this was true.

Returning from the war I was easily distracted, I felt as though my mind was always operating in high gear and I was never really present in the "here and now." It was as if my body sought to be on a new path, but my mind and spirit were still in a war zone. In hindsight, I was lost, distorted, and most of all, distracted. My intuition was scrambled and my passions or motivation were out of my control and not focused in any one direction. I was no longer one with myself, with my higher faculties, or with God. I was neither whole nor in the "Dao." Lao Tzu says: "Riding and hunting make our minds wild and our hearts turn mad," (Chapter 12 verse 4). That is what I had been doing for the last four years in the Army and that is exactly how I felt. Congressperson Barbara Lee once exclaimed when voting against a 2014 Military Authorization Bill: "as we act, let us not become the evil we deplore." It was as if she could glimpse into the dark side of my motivation.

My life was full of disharmony, almost as if I were fighting an evil disease or that I was living a life of sin in the sense that according to Eckhart Tolle the meaning of "sin" is "missing one's mark." According to the Chinese, evil is an imbalance in oneself, occurring when one is living backwards (Is it by chance that "live" spelled backwards is "evil"?) Lao Tzu again says: "The only way to rid oneself of a disease is to be sick of it."

As an outlet, I spent several years after the Army training and fighting in martial arts. After winning several events I decided to take my quest east to train in Thailand and to continue my education in China. It was in the library of the Peking

University's Classical Studies Department that I found a bit of solace, a place where I could decompress and reflect on my experiences in combat and in martial arts. In my head I felt a bit like "Conan The Barbarian" after he had proven himself in battle and then, receiving a great prize, was sent to the Far East, to learn the poetry of Khitai, the philosophy of Sung, and the secrets of the war masters. It was during this time at Peking University that I became obsessed with classical Chinese texts like the I-Ching and consumed with the goal of discovering the secrets to life and achieving my Dao. I believed that by discovering the Dao I would not only find my own way but perhaps one day help others in finding theirs.

The traditional I-Ching requires divination: the use of coins, yarrows, or staves in order to receive an answer to a question from the Oracle by inspection of randomly tossed binary hexagrams. Each of the I-Ching's 64 hexagrams represent a changing "element." My hypothesis is that the top two lines represent both 'God' or 'The Dao' and one's intuition; the middle two lines, where Heaven and Earth meet, represent the heart or spirit; and the bottom two lines represent the body and the path that the practitioner is currently on.

The I-Ching is a guide to help one not just find her way, but to enhance it by giving its practitioners a deeper understanding of and connection with the changes in life. It is important for the practitioner to understand that there are some things (certain cycles in life) that are out of the practitioner's control, and that it is a waste of energy to try to change them. But at the same time, action is sometimes called for: there are other things in the practitioner's life that can be confronted to yield good or bad outcomes. At these ties, the practitioner may meet others who are on the same path but who have different ultimate destinations. One purpose of the I-Ching is to guide the practitioner through these challenges.

Ironically, sometimes the very path that the practitioner has chosen in order to *avoid* one's fate ends up being a shortcut to that destined outcome. That's called an "inverted change" or destiny. According to Chinese interpreters of the I-Ching, some things in this life are fated for a certain individual and accepting that fate becomes one of the practitioner's highest virtues. The practitioner who encounters repeated and seemingly unavoidable quarrels or dilemmas may end up coming to an understanding and acceptance of the reality that these experiences have been mapped out by fate and that the best approach is to go through it.

I believe the I-Ching is a tool to aid in recalibrating the practitioner's innate life compass. It fulfills man's natural need to know the future, but this knowledge can only play out within a human context, not in a way that belongs only to divination. Once you understand and are able to identify the elements of change in your life, and if you have the courage to take right actions, you will have little or no need for further divination, nor will you need to fear the future: "If God is for me, who can be against me?" (Romans 8:3). The successful practitioner of the I-Ching comes into alignment across three dimensions: he is aligned with himself, with his God, and with his Dharma or purpose in life (his Dao). Lao Tzu teaches us that the Dao promotes benevolence, righteousness and cultivating loyalty to oneself in order to live a life with dignity and integrity. Jordan Peterson once said, "Be a good person! There is no better life strategy."

This book is entitled "The Art of War Within" because I believe all of its readers — all of humanity — deal with one or more underlying conflicts. We are all warfighters.

What is your war? What bothers you? What are you afraid of? In my life, it happened to be readjusting to civilian life after the military, facing a painful breakup, and struggling with use of a controlled substance. The wisdom conveyed by the I-Ching taught me, and will also teach you, that such conflicts invariably point to problems having to do with change: change occurring within, change coming from the outside, or sometimes change that ultimately needs to be understood and merely accepted. It is my hope that my epigrammatic rendering of the Book of Changes will help you to identify, penetrate, find meaning, and creatively respond to the changes that you experience.

Introduction

The challenge confronting the modern reader of millennia-old texts is to successfully (or at least adequately) recontextualize them within contemporary settings, thereby making them accessible without sacrificing their essential meanings. This introduction briefly discusses three classical texts: The Art of War, the 36 strategies, I-Ching, and The Tao. Its ultimate aim is to arrive at an epigrammatic reformulation of the 64 elements of the I-Ching in order to make that millennia-old text more readily available when confronting life's vicissitudes.

This introduction briefly discusses Sun Tzu's Art of War for essentially autobiographical reasons. Like millions before me, I approached "The Art of War" (from here on AOW) hoping to find a "cure all" for dealing with life's multiple facets, especially with problems arising from conflict with others, whether a single antagonist, or with many others in a larger social environment, or even—especially in capitalist America — deployment in order to gain a competitive edge in the world of business.

My early uses of "AOW" were fundamentally instrumental, and as such they manifested the materialism that defines Western culture. I and many other users perceived "AOW" to be about engaging in direct combat with the opposition in order to strong arm an opponent through the direct and indirect application of force. A telling indicator of this materialist point of view is that readers approach the text as mostly a "book of black magic" or the source of some supernatural "death touch" that enables its practitioner to "go after," "outsmart," conquer, or dominate all opponents through deception, manipulation, and trickery.

At least, that is what I thought the "AOW" was going to accomplish for me at age 11 when I opened Thomas Cleary's "Mastering the Art of War". My juvenile expectations about what this text would offer me were, I believe, not unlike those of most western students of classical Chinese literature. The materialism and empiricism of western culture ill equips western readers for truly understanding the wisdom with which they attempt to engage. In my case, it wasn't until 16 years later, while studying the Chinese language at Peking University (and later at Tsinghua University) that I began to gain insight into what the "AOW" was, and more importantly, what it was not.

How then does a "non materialist" perspective differ? First, multiple readings of Sun Tzu's 13 chapters slowly reveal that "AOW," far from encouraging conflict or battle, instead offers a paradigm (in Silicon Valley jargon, a flowchart or algorithm) for calculating or assessing the chances of success *while not necessarily going to war.* Sun Tzu clearly states that waging war and applying violence, even when necessary, is always "costly" for both sides:

"To win one hundred victories in one hundred battles is not the acme of skill. To subdue the enemy without fighting is the acme of skill."

Later, Sun Tzu adds: "Strategy without tactics is the slowest route to victory. Tactics without strategy is the noise before defeat."

This insight from "AOW" motivated me to ask the question "Is there another book that has stratagems and tactics listed?" If "The Art of War" was a flowchart or algorithm that once learned required information regarding tactics, then "San Shi Liu-Ji" or "The Book of the 36 Stratagems" becomes an obvious stepping stone. "The 36 Stratagems" is a collection of strategies set down by military leaders, politicians, and philosophers. Divided into six categories, each with six strategies, the text addresses topics such as: tactics when one is in a superior position, in a confrontation, in attacking, in confusing situations, for gaining ground, and when in desperate straits. After reading "The 36 Stratagems," I came to the realization that all choices among strategies require an awareness of and response to *change*: to be able to choose the right tactic for the right time; to adapt to your opponent's way of thinking; to adapt to the weather or to the terrain, etc. Ultimately, I concluded that the answer to the question "What is Strategy?" is that it consists of the study of the uses of and responses to *change*. I also concluded that a deep understanding of *change* (especially in terms of the cycles emphasized in Chinese culture as compared to the emphasis on the linear in Western culture) might even allow one to *forecast* future events.

This conclusion motivated my turn to the Yi-Jing or Book of Changes, a philosophy that predates the AOW by at least 3000 years. After using the Yi-Jing for many years, I have observed that the text covers three types of change: Cyclical, polar, and inverted changes. The Yi-Jing also posits the notion of the Yin and Yang, and the harmonies that emerge from the two. This ultimate balancing is also referred to as "The Dao" or "The Way." The Dao promotes self-cultivation and the necessity of walking one's own path, so that by doing so one can live a long or short but fulfilled life. Taken together, the Yi-Jing and the Dao invite us, when we are in conflict with something or someone else, to first ask the question: "Are we in conflict *with ourselves* and with our Dao?"

When seen together, there is an interesting and productive interplay between the perspectives found in these key texts. They suggest that the ultimate goal for a person is to discover their Dao and live it. By doing so, an enlightened agent does not have to resort to applying wiles, schemes, stratagems and ruses. In fact, resorting to maneuvers aimed at confusing and manipulating others in order to gain success is tantamount to self destruction. Lao Tzu tells us that "the more clever the strategy, the stranger the outcome." I believe that the true focus of the "AOW" is to mobilize the wisdom in the Yi-Jing towards the only war that matters: the war we wage within ourselves. The project proposed here is, through the use of epigrammatic summaries of the Yi-Jing's 64 elements, to aid in recognizing and mastering the elements of the Yi-Ching so that we can thereby discern the challenges we encounter in our everyday lives and by applying principles of the Dao, master our lives by mastering ourselves.

How to Use This Book

Each epigram was written to explain what elemental change is occurring and why, along with how to deal with the change. The epigrams were written to rhyme so that the practitioner can easily remember, recite, and recall its teaching.

The following acronym MR DAO explains the proposed exercise for the reader.

M - Memorize each epigram or the one that resonates with you.

R - Recite each epigram.

D - Discern your situation daily to the appropriate epigram which it relates to.

A - Analyze by asking yourself What is Occurring and why? .

O - Operate with the epigram's suggested prescription.

Element 1: Creative Power 乾

A warrior must strengthen the Will.
Like heaven with its untring Power.
Casting out all that is inferior and all that degrades
Refining the spirit, hour by hour.

Avoid aspirations that exceed your true ability.
Be mild in action and strong in decision.
Integrity and Dignity can be destroyed by over ambition.

Dangers lurk in the transitions between lowliness and great heights.
Do not expend your light prematurely;
Using unguided Force to obtain that which is unripe.

Element II: Natural Response 坤

A warrior allows for guidance.
There are times you must not push boldly ahead.

Reality requires strength and swiftness,
Spirituality; gentleness and devotion.
Be reserved with discretion
Use non-action and strength in proper proportion.

Conceal your abilities and do not feel perturbed.
Not attracting attention too soon
Allows your powers to mature undisturbed.

Acknowledge solitude with acceptance;
It is the intimation of the Fates.
It is your period of Purity unspoiled
Protection from factional hates.

Like a seed residing alone
Deep in dark soil.
Solitude is its sacred space:
For there is purity in toil.

Element III: Difficult Beginnings 屯

Beginnings contain raw elements of profusion;
Dark and unformed, resembling chaos and confusion.

Masters manifest by being concerned how events are born;
He discerns the seeds of coming events.
Keeping his goals in sight he weathers the storm.

Element IV: Inexperience 蒙

A young warrior's folly is common but rarely evil.
However, continued conscious foolishness can lead to
Misfortune and upheaval.

Seek an avatar who does not want to be sought;
Who teaches discipline yet encourages free thought.

A teacher who encourages your natural ability.
One who never punishes out of anger!
Yet he is one who restores a student's humility.

Be devoid of arrogance and you will always be helped.
Adopt the attitude of a childlike man;
Then teachers will guide and guard you like a lion's whelp.

Element V: Calculated Waiting 需

Waiting guards against wasting strength
The profusion of elements is unclear.
Nourish and strengthen until circumstances are in your favor.
Worrying only causes inward confusion, chaos, and fear.
This time is meant to test your commitment and faith.
Destiny is at work here.

Element VI: Conflict 訟

Enemies, obstacles, and opponents you must respect.
It could be that your path and purpose along with their view and position are equally correct.

Aggressive and cunning strategies will always bring about evil and corruption.
Causing imbalance within will weaken your power to conquer outside disruption.

To retreat when the enemy is stronger is no disgrace.
Subdue your ego, bury your pride, relinquish your need to save face.

A righteous one should not contend
Even a sincere individual will fail
If he pursues evil to the bitter end.

True unity cannot be won with forceful measures.
This may be a time for spiritual maturing.
One of life's unseen developments, one of life's hidden treasures.

Element VII: Collective Force 師

Like groundwater stored deep within the Earth lies a warrior's source.
He must discipline this potential danger by harnessing and directing its force.

In times of peace this strength must remain hidden and tamed.
In times of war using it with correctness, and discipline will bring about righteous aims.

This uncontrolled force can bring about destruction and devastation.
Any misuse or overuse and you will suffer defeat and disintegration.

War begins and every peasant becomes a soldier.
They must be used carefully and considerately with everyone taking a vow.
When the war ends everyone returns to their duties, every farmer, his plow.

At the end
every faculty returns to its norms.
Until this Force is needed again
You will feel and control its changes
command its growth inside you as it informs.

Element VIII: Unity 比

A warrior of great strength and Will is the center of unity.
Bringing and holding people together should not be done imprudently.
A man of great spirit is one of consistency
Never clever with words he speaks with sincerity

He responds reservedly and in the right way;
Acting with dignity, not losing himself, not going astray.

He is cautious of those who do not belong in his sphere.
Aware of false intimacy he prevents chaos and evil from entering.
The elements that destroy relationships and make matters unclear.

Element IX: Gentle Restraint 小畜

A small obstacle can restrain and impede.
Only gentle determination and adaptability succeed.
This is a time to refine the expression of your nature and deeds.

Strong men that push forward encounter obstruction in their course
Sometimes even wise men do not always obtain their objective by force.

To push forward one must be in harmony with the pressures of time
Until then retreat with others of like spirit and like mind

Be content with what you have achieved no matter how small the portion
Advancing further before the appropriate time will result in misfortune.

Element X: Conduct 履

Sometimes safety and danger reside with one another.
A clumsy man will step on a tiger's tail
He acts with propriety and pleasant manners,
His humor is harmless and he remains unassailed.

He is simple, seeking nor asking nothing
Un-dazzled by enticing goals
He travels on a level road
Without exacting the burden of heavy tolls

Task beyond his strength he does not undertake
He is free from entanglement
because he does not interfere with his nature's Fate.

Element XI: Harmony 泰

When things are in harmony they bloom and prosper.
There is a time when even evil elements change for the better.
An equal exchange between heaven and earth is unfettered.

When the spirit of heaven rules and shines through man's face.
He regulates this gift
Placing Primal instincts and natures in their appropriate place.

Like a new awakening filled with fertile earth
He who can regulate this rich beginning shapes his futures birth

Remember, Evil is never abolished, it always returns, so be mindful of danger.
He who makes use of the useless is useful, making use of even hate and anger.

Element XII: Stagnation 否

A time when Heaven and Earth draw further apart.
They are disjointed and disunited.
Affairs are benumbed
Confusion reigns and disorder is now expedited.

A warrior withdraws
Calmly bearing and enduring his principles
Finding safety and security in seclusion.
They do not allow themselves to ascend with inferior people
Willingness to suffer alone brings victory against disillusion.

To be honored during an evil time will expose you to danger.
Do not mingle with inferior people. Give them their space.
Inferior people readily flatter their superiors with servility.
They rise illegitimately with their hearts ashamed and abased

Success is secured through caution of the elements waiting to befoul.
Never forget that danger destruction and ruin are always on prowl

Element XIII: Fellowship 同人

Everyone in society has their place.
A craft to contribute regardless of age color creed or race

A leader is needed for the continuing of a community
Free of self-serving motives, his only interest is unity

He recognizes the talents of others
Organizes them by rank, order, and character of deeds

Bringing people together, one in their inmost hearts
More than mere mingling he fulfills all their needs.

Element XIV: Sovereignty 大有

Enjoy prosperity on top of nature's abundance.
Maintain your humbleness and you will be blessed
Modesty brings fortune, material wealth, and success.

Pose no threat
Gain loyalty and obedience from those above and below
Proper behavior is necessary
For accomplishments to continue to flow.

Find Compassion
Find the weakness of others in yourself is the way to save face
Compassion is the way to keep ego, greed, and pride in their place.

Element XV: Modesty 謙

Nature balances using plagues and famine
Balancing the overpowering and overabundant
Causing human nature to strive for moderation
To rid excess and extremes, to reduce the over redundant

The law of heaven is to make fullness empty
To make emptiness full
A person can shape fate with behavior
Allowing humility and modesty be your savior

In a high position
Modesty shines with wisdom
In a lowly
It is never passed by

Hard work earns a distinguished name
Difficulties arise only for those in pursuit of fame.

Do not mistake modesty for weakness!

A passive one with no course
Modest is one who is Mighty
Who has courage and strength
To Marshal one's inner force

Element XVI: Enthusiasm 豫

Rivers rush down to fill the oceans
Feel the directions and tendencies around you
These are the worlds emotions

Parallel them to accomplish your deeds
Penetrate the popular sentiment of societies needs

Least resistance is nature's order
From oceans tides to earth's gravity
Wars shatter spirits
Bringing disharmony and depravity

Element XVII: Adapting 隨

Life survives the seasons by adapting
Insects burrow and animals hibernate

There is a time to act and a time to rest
A time to speak, a time for silence
Times of peace and times of violence

Element XVIII: Repair 蠱

We all have weak points, unaware
A time of decay, collapse
A state of disrepair

You have been injured
Struck in your Achilles Heel
Self incurred wounds
Only you can heal

Do not be lulled into inertia
Recoil and the danger will spread
A spoiled state abuse of freedom
Corruption originating from neglect

Element XIX: Promotion 臨

Work and faith bring promotion which is followed by decline;
Like spring after winter seasons mark the cycles of time.

What goes up must come down a descent follows every rise
This universal law should not be taken as a surprise.

To master the paths of life one must meet evil before it begins;
He who heeds the change of time swiftly, and honestly, valiantly wins.

Element XX: Contemplation 觀

The laws of heaven and earth
Subject to the cyclical laws of life

Spring of inspiration, summer of work
Autumn of completion, winter of contemplation

A person of great faith can master himself
With Holy seriousness and deep concentration

Mysterious and divine laws he can apprehend
This kind of person cannot be deceived
A spiritual power emanates from him

His ability to predict and master the world
With him no one can contend
He sways people
Like grass by the wind

Element XXI: Reform 噬嗑

An inferior person stands in your way
A powerful hardened sinner aroused by evil
This person must be reformed or eliminated
Before causing permanent damage and upheaval

Usually a talebearer or traitor
Deceiving the hearts
Manipulating the laws of men
They will not escape the eyes of God
Or the nets of heaven

In the end
Punishments and penalties must be certain and swift
You must be hard as steel and straight as an arrow
To protect yourself be correct
Walk the path of the straight and narrow

Element XXII: Grace 賁

Still, and pleasing to the heart
This moment is a state of Grace
Inside a protected vessel your sacred space

Time to shape your world
A time to reflect and to refine
Your life unfolds in this inspiring time

Make no major decisions
When your desires are silenced
The Will comes to rest
Upon which your future will unfold
And manifest

Element XXIII: Deterioration 剥

The Dark Forces have overcome the strong
They began their destruction by burrowing
Danger draws near
Powers of evil people are growing

These people move stealthily
Undermining imperceptibility until collapse
Destroying with slander and intrigue
Wherever the superion person elapse

It is not cowardice but wisdom to submit
Remain quiet all one can do is wait
Evil is a "timed" condition
A law of heaven a test of fate

Respect cycles of increase and decrease
Greatness and decadence
Concern yourself only with yourself
Protect loved ones with intelligence

Sometimes darkness is impossible to counteract
Time itself will put an end to corruption
Negativity is self consuming
Evil always ends in sudden irruption.

Element XXIV: Returning 復

A turning point in your life
A second chance
The time of darkness has passed
Victory and light arrive at last

After being halted at every turn
After a long period of stagnation
A new sense of profound inner knowledge
A time free of frustration

Cyclic courses in nature complete itself
Movement not forced or induced
Old is discarded and the new introduced

Element XXV: Innocence 無妄

There are those
Directed by a spirit of innocence, life fulfills their demand;
There are those who can draw spiritual wealth on command.

Pure of heart, intention, and purpose
This person summons heaven's hand

Cleverness, plots and plans end in difficulty and confusion
The innocent make adjustments without guile and obtrusion.

Element XXVI: Potential Energy 大畜

A great amount of psychic energy
A time of vast importance
Able to undertake a far reaching endeavor
This timing will not last forever

This psychic energy is directed and tamed
Your creativity is strong and clear headed
Your personality should be in harmony with heaven
Honored is the person with firmness and truth embedded

A storehouse of mental power is a hidden treasure
It should be used to elevate and strengthen your character
A man untamed should be combatted indirectly and uprooted
He is unworthy of great power and unsuited

A mans whos principles are unfurled
He prevails and his vision shapes the world

Element XXVII: Nourishment 頤

Tend to yourself with care and nourishing.
Foster only worthy people and goals worth flourishing.
Nourish your positive nature
Cultivate your character traits worthy of praise
Protect yourself from all things that cause malaise

To know people observe them
How and to whom they bestow their care
With this caution you can avoid many snares
What goes in and out of their mouth
Reflect on their negative natures and forswear

Element XXVIII: Critical Mass 大過

You will encounter a times when all of the forces of your life collide
The weight of the world is too great and there will be nowhere to hide.

Evaluate all of the things affecting you with transition in mind
Remain strong and certain within,
confidence and courageousness will keep you unbind

Be prepared to take your stand!
Resilience of your character will see you through.
You may have to face this time alone
Do so, and renounce your entire milieu.

At times it is better to stand alone
Renouncing the world and remaining undaunted.
This will clear your path leaving you redeemed and unhaunted.

Element XXIX: Danger 坎

Danger and strife are essential ingredients of life;
One must know when to run and when to hide and when to fight.

Only fools and harlots dally with danger for thrill
A warrior meets danger with confidence, virtue, and skill.

Sometimes to keep harm away one must keep danger close.
Confront danger with the silence and stillness of a ghost.

Like death, danger can bring profound awareness, insight, and depth.
Adding meaning and richness to your life within every breath.

Element XXX: Synergy 離

A person who rises to quickly is sure to wreck;
Like a meteor that consumes itself, he leaves no lasting effect.

Passing moods versus change of heart one should construe.
Align your goals with the energies of the events around you.

The evolved soul cares not whether or death comes early or late;
A true warrior works quietly, diligently, with only her soul to cultivate.
He foresees his future faults thereby securing his fate.

Element XXXI: Attraction 咸

A profound attraction exist
Between you and a person of interest

People are dangerous
They plot, plan, and scheme
Examine this persons nature
Their energies, ideas, and dreams

Will they benefit you?
Pay attention to what their nature attracts
Judgment concerning another based on facts

Penetrate their fate
Do they use their influence to manipulate?
Is their timing in life bad
With whom they associate?
Will this benefit you?

Element XXXII: Enduring 恆

Thunder rolls and the wind blows
Success is reserved for the committed.
For the warrior willing to pay its toll.

Trust your instincts when choosing a direction
Be mindful of the times.
Maintain your principles while growing and adapting.
Like a trellis and its vines.

Element XXXIII: Retreat 遯

The moment reaches its fullness with darkness rising
One must prepare to retreat
Interpreting the signs wisely doing so with accurate timing.

Retreat too soon and never return, wait too long and be trapped
A warrior does not push forward, he is composed and ready to adapt.

Retreating inward keeping silent and still to escape defeat
With Absolute firmness of decision
Strength is gained through retreat

Element XXXIV: Great Power 大壯

Great Power is bestowed upon you
The truest test of character
Your words are heard
Your thoughts are felt
Concern yourself with correctness of matters dealt

Inappropriate actions will put you into chaos
Your Power will not last!
If you implement good works, you will not go unnoticed
Even when your Power has passed.

In personal relationships
Power is not a luxury but a responsibility
Be mindful of your shortcomings
Be a leader of action with humility

Boasting leads to entanglements
Do not rely on yourself completely
Do not rely on one-sided sight
Appoint noble and wise men
Do not be afraid to ask what is right

True greatness is
To be in harmony with heaven and earth
Inwardly united with righteousness and justice
When you are right you will fear nothing
No need for excessive force, pushing or rushing.

Element XXXV: Progression 晉

A time of rapid progress and radiance
You serve others with your intelligence

Supported and emulated by those in authority
You are recognized and given prominence
Your virtue is rewarded with intimacy and confidence

Because of your influence, humility, and fidelity
Those above you remain free of envy
Suspicion and jealousy

However,
There are times great possession amass the wrong man
They must be undone and brought to light by a strong man.

Element XXXVI: Censorship 明夷

The Sun has sunken
Your light is wounded
By Darkness you are surrounded

Confronted by a person of Dark nature
Evil and sable.
They are in the position of Power
They bring harm to the wise and able.

The righteous are confronted
Their convictions threatened
Use your intelligence by hiding it
Concealment is your greatest weapon

Accept Good and Evil
Like Night and Day

Act not with enmity
The Darkness will reveal its thoughts
Hold to a fierce inner awareness
You will evade the disaster evil plots

Element XXXVII: Family 家人

Husband and Wife
Are like Heaven and Earth
A father is a man's greatest worth

Well being of the family is first
Taking care of the roots
Family comes before individual pursuits

Bring your house to order
Stability brings loyalty to leaders
Faithfulness and obedience
Words of power and clarity

Avoid that which you are unsuited
It will rob your life of meaning
Never seek anything by force
Govern your family with love
Fear and severity only brings remorse

A father has a richly endowed mind
His work commands respect He is trusted
In him they conform and confine

Element XXXVIII: Contradiction and Opposition 睽

Contradiction occurs when opposition appears
Divergent forces, and inner dualities bring about indecision

Only small endeavors and gradual influences succeed
Great ideals and achievements will be met with opposition

Struggles between life and death, good and evil
Trying to rid of evil men by force will give rise to hostility

They must be endured
It will seem as if all is conspiring against you
You will feel check and hindered in futility

Your progress unsuited and dishonored
Nose and hair severed with unanimity
Perhaps you have found someone with an inner affinity?

No discord, No concord
Through an exchange of blows
Your relationship grows
When contradiction is at its worst
Opposition will ebb and flow

Element XXXIX: Obstacles 蹇

When paths are blocked your journey pauses;
As within so without, sometimes external obstacles come from internal causes.

The superior man knows that to blame others is to bewail his fate;
To seek error within is the only way to extricate.

However, some are restricted by fate to climb a perilous steep.
Pulled purposely into the turmoil of life to create something great.
Beyond your understanding, to make work of a higher cause complete.

Element XL: Deliverance 解

To move in and out of dangers sphere
To make tensions and complications disappear

Matters of great importance have sudden change
Like atmospheric tensions, resentments are relieved by the rain.

A true warrior pardons mistakes and forgives misdeeds
Not overdoing triumph is an act of good breed.

What happens in the past we cannot elude
His greatest weapon comes from his rectitude.

Element XLI: Decline 損

This is the decline of power
This is a natural cycle of space and time

Self-made sacrifices benefit you when your power is declining
Sincerity and simplicity will improve your sense of timing

Stubborn strength creates anger,
resisting decline makes one's reality distorted
To pretend you are living in opulent times
This causes character to become contorted.

Time in Hell is dependent on your resistance to decline
Heaven and Hell are both here on Earth
Decline is the essential
A transitional stage to rebirth.

Element XLII: Increase 益

Positive energy
Directed your way
A time of increase rest assured
It cannot last or be endured

Do not be heedless
Acquire meaning before God
That which you strive for
Will arrive like flowerey sod

Sometimes an unfortunate event
Is a blessing in disguise
God's rejection is God's protection
Keeping away your own demise

A kind heart is rewarded and recognized
For its charity and zeal
Such inner authority
Exerting great influence
As if sanctioned by letter and seal

If you give
Give without thought of your own gain
Do not give what you do not have
It will bring indignity, suffering, and pain

Element XLIII: Resolution 夬

Evil must be eradicated.
Forces that threaten your position.

To engage your adversaries
you acknowledge their strengths.
You give them power.
Deny their power making a resolution
Grow in the direction of good.

Corrupt motives, selfish interest or
Hidden deceptions bring failure

Evil brandishes its weapons
Without opposing force
They grow dull

Guard against the unseen;
Victory leaves behind a remnant of
evil

Let reason triumph so that passion
withdraws

Element XLIV: Temptation 姤

A darkness has returned
Evil can never be fully eliminated
Disguised as a harmless element
Innocent Yet Ill-fated

A bold girl who surrenders lightly
Seeming harmless
inviting and smiling delightfully
A usurpers that secretly scours
Creating darkness seizing control and power

Or a new indulgence
An internal temptation difficult to sway
Creating more problems than profits
Requires a demanding character to turn it away

Element XLV: Assembling 萃

Shared bonds
A state or nation
Secret forces lead together
Those who belong together
Family or religious congregation

Honorable and trustworthy
Commitment and loyalty
From the center the leader leads
Only a collective and moral force
Will succeed
Causing unity and movement
Towards greater deeds

Great men gather
Great strength and number
All of likemind
Twined together
They leave great achievements
behind

If untwined
Strife will arise
Where valuables reside
Thieves and robbers will
Abide
Arms are needed to ward off evil
To fend for the unprotected
Human woes come from
The unseen
The unexpected

Element XLVI: Advancement 升

Personal power is in timely accord
All your work should be centered with the Will
Through a steady Will your luck will remain
With unwavering effort your successes will gain

During great times remain sober!
Skip no pages, stages, or steps.
Do not become intoxicated by success
Stop before your cup begins to spillover
A calm and steady metamorphosis

Pushing upward blindly deludes
Knowing only advance and not retreat
Only brings exhaustion and vision skewed

Element XLVII: Adversity 困

The right man understands that adversity is success in reverse.
His attitude alone can turn to a blessing within what seems like a curse.

He remains cheerful despite the danger
He remains firm in the face of oppression
Reconnecting with his soul during the state of depression

He stakes his life on his Will
His actions and his deeds will allow him to succeed

This too shall pass
With patience of Spirit events are endured
He overcomes outward trouble inwardly
His negative thoughts are cured

He does not let his spirit break
With stability he masters himself
At that moment he is stronger than fate.

Element XLVIII: The Source 井

A spiritual wellspring
Filled with the Divine
The town can change
But the Well cannot

Set your mind on humanity
You will be free of evil

Generations come and go
The Spirit of Truth remains
If a leader is not the right man
Evil will reign

Men differ in disposition
Men differ in education
But human nature all the same

Ignoring your good qualities
Will deteriorate your mind
Put your life in order first
Accomplish more at a later time

Element XLIX: Revolution 革

Conflict
Creates a chance for change
Inadvertently
People fear not knowing
Change comes with uncertainty

Times change
So do the demands of the time
Changes requires utmost restraint
To be firm in one's mind

If change comes to one's ear
Three time repeated
The warning should be heeded
Hesitation only brings disaster
Transformation is needed

Element L: The Cauldron 鼎

For the devoted
Fate lends power to your life
Personality and motivation aligned
Fulfilling the needs of the world
This is the meaning of Divine

Ideals in accord with the cosmos are effortlessly rewarded;
When not, your plans are easily thwarted.

Certain areas of your life and nature are fated
Acceptance of these earthly limits is how great personal power is created.

Awareness of this allows you to grow and develop beyond the physical
To the depths of your soul
The spirit world, realm of the invisible.

Achievement always brings about envy and disfavor
Be modest in nature
Mild and pure finding favor

Element LI: Shocking 震

Kinetic energy released
A experience causing reverence and fear
This is the presence of God drawing near

An unpredictable cataclysmic occurrence
Movement of invisible forces
Symbolized by thunder and lightning
Bringing a new awareness both heightening and frightening

Fear God!
A new turn of events
Know in your heart
What fear and trembling mean
Fearing God will safeguard you
Against whatever outside terrors may bring.

Element LII: Stillness 艮

Focus requires stillness
A listening frame of mind
With Meditation your ego is quelled
Your life can then be realigned

Center yourself
To transcend inner turmoil
Know when to act and when to not
Inner peace amongst outer complexities
Virtue frees one from anxieties
Wisdom one from perplexities
Projecting too far into the future
Dispels the present creating difficulties

Shut the door of your desires
Be vacuous
Be not the storehouse of schemes
Be not the possessor of fame
Achieve a quiet heart
Still and tamed

Acting from these depths
You will make to mistakes
The heart thinks mans thoughts
Forcing Smothers and suffocates
Step back rest and yield
Overthinking makes the heart sore
Halt until the path is revealed

Element LIII: Developing 漸

The time seems slow and unchallenging
A careful and slow cultivation with events still developing.

It could be a time of maturing.
Like a tree that grew slowly.
It is firmly rooted deeply

Its flowers and fruits ripening
Tranquility guarded it
against interruptions and stifling

A safe place, an inner calm.
The law of non-interference
Knowing when to stop
This is where life goes on

Element LIV: Subordinate 歸妹

Life is unrewarding
You are dependent on situation of circumstance
Everything you do, inappropriate
It has never been easier for you to make mistakes
Subordinate.
All you can do is wait.

You perceive your difficulties
You have control over none
No one is interested in your views
Withdraw into the background
This is your time to shun

Strengthen your inner vision
A long-term Ideal
This will take you beyond this time
Clarity of purpose for a future plan
Circumstances do not make but instead reveal the man.

Element LV: Zenith 豐

Greatness and Abundance

Every mortal cannot attain.
A modest ruler with counsel
Is needed to maintain

For the commoner
Wealth is usually brief
Abundance quickly reaches its peak
Anxiously anticipating poverty
His future is scarce and bleak

Do not try to persevere the zenith of greatness
Do not be eclipsed at the height of the climb
Decline is a natural cycle of life and time

Element LVI: Traveler 旅

You wake up and find yourself in a distant land.
You have no roots, a tourist of life,

A stranger searching, tasting, testing,
A wanderer sightseeing and collecting.

Search for good paths. Be helpful and humble.
Behave with manners and modesty, proprietary and grace.
Cautiousness and reserve will protect you from evil and disgrace.

This may be an inner voyage
A walking target with no fixed home.
Take care your actions
The road is your humble abode.

Element LVII: Penetrating Influence 巽

Influence
Penetrating winds
Subliminal messages sent
Ceaselessness never lapping
Time is its effective
Invisible instrument

Mountains are eroded and sculpted
Twisting trees into exotic shapes serene
Clouds disperse across the sky clearly
All inspired by the wind unseen

A profound effect of the steady
Gradual efforts and consistent direction
Emulating the Gentle and unceasing

Speak sweet sentiments of your goal in mind
Patience and commitment to your vision
Concentration and attention to your intention
Bringing about through the power of mind

Element LVIII: Encouraging Joy 兌

Encouragement
Brings great joy
Great powers over men
Inspiring them to great heights
Even the fear of death they transcend.
Knowledge
Is firm truth at the center
Refreshing and revitalizing force
Knowing, learning, and teaching
Bring about stimulating intercourse.
Brings wisdom to the heart
Which brings about protection
Happinesses' counterpart
Happiness
Can be preserved or reserved
True joy rest on firmness
Strength from within
Coming from one's work
Born from exhaustion
Do not become frivolous
Losing yourself in joy
False intimacy and optimism
Bring about obligation and cloy
Joy can be silence
To desire nothing
To be alone and unsung
Stability equals freedom
A wellspring sprung.
Dangerous elements approach the best of men
Idle pleasures bringing disaster in its train. Decide and seal it!
Do not give up your life to chance. Nature does nothing in vain.

Element LIX: Dispersion 渙

Factions dissolve and commitments to common causes fall in line.
In life these are powerful moments of time.

Isolation can also bring discord and cause fatality
Elitism and egotism cut the stream of creativity
Break up that which divides and reunite with reality.

Element LX: Limitations 節

Water in a lake
Occupying a limited space
Man must set fixed limits on his actions
Thrift with money and emotions
Curbing extremes in promises and passions

Limits of Summer
Day and Night
Limits give meaning

Unlimited possibilities are unsuited for man
His life would dissolve into the boundless
With no restraints or commitments
Man is Overwhelmed with possibilities
His goals become shapeless and soundless

Stopping he accumulates energy
Enabling him to act with great force
Only imposing limits on himself
Only himself should he enforce
To overcome temptation
To save his soul
Ruthlessness is his recourse

Element LXI: Insight 中孚

Insight
The Sage has the abielity to understand difficult matters clearly
This is greater than any physical might.
One's mind must remain open and unprejudiced
Accepting the pressures of time and the light.

Correct character establishes contact with the invisible factions
Embodying another's spirit you become a vessel of empathy, a spiritual attraction.
Your inner strength and character shape events and influence others actions

Choosing to live quietly in good health or lead others to live their true vision
This person's words and deeds can bring heaven to submission.

Element LXII: Conscientiousness 小過

Remain low and modest
Bring about your life's work

Do not strive for flamboyant or lofty things
Complete your ordinary duty with attention to detail
no matter how petty it may seem

Ponder the small
To contemplating delicacy brings about humility
Pride leads you away from insights and towards debility.

Be not like those who do not stop and can
Who deviate from the true order of nature
Who draws upon himself misfortune
from both the hands of God and man.

Element LXIII: After the End 既濟

Dangers lurk before, during and after the end.
The time calls for inner caution and fortification. .
If anything can go wrong it will.
Forethought and vigilance will arm you against misfortune.

Overshooting your goal will lead to loss and collapse.
After completion people grow intoxicated with arrogance
Conceit leads to the lessons lost and negativity relapsed.

Move forward and do not look back!
You will escape danger.
There is a fascination to look back at the peril overcome.
This vain self-admiration brings misfortune.
One must be Resolved to move forward.
Once and for all
Done

Element LXIV: Before the End 未濟

The journey incomplete yet the goal is in sight
No matter the mark
It is most dangerous near the end
It is always darkest before the light

Leading the world out of chaos and confusion
Establishing a new order

Prepare with wariness and reserve
Use patience to investigate the forces in question
Before the final pieces of chaos come into order
Evaluate and arrange with your successes preserved

Paul Justin Tiemujin Ramirez is a US Army Combat Veteran, Horatio Alger Military Scholar, and a graduate from Peking University's advanced Chinese language immersion program. He holds a B.A. degree in Chinese language and literature with an emphasis in Chinese strategic culture from Cal State University Los Angeles. You may contact him at: artofwarwithin@gmail.com

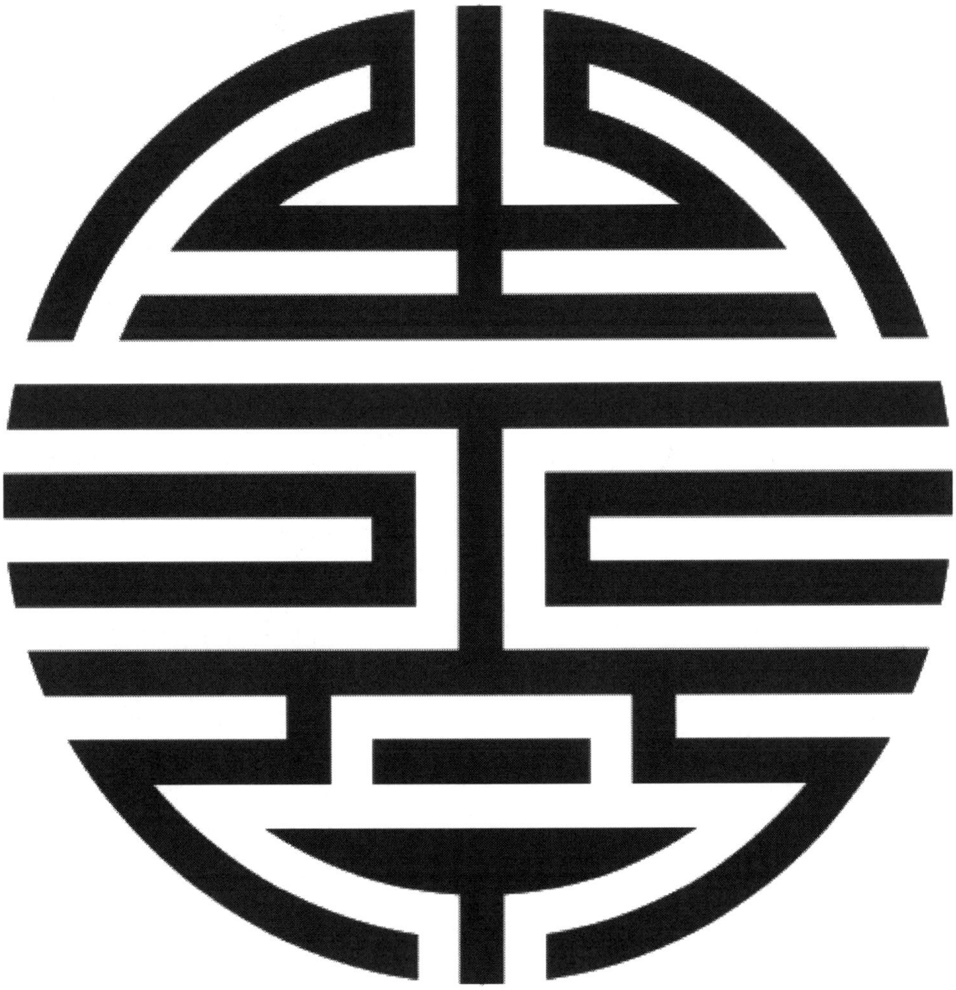